# LOVEBITES

SANDEEP DAHIYA

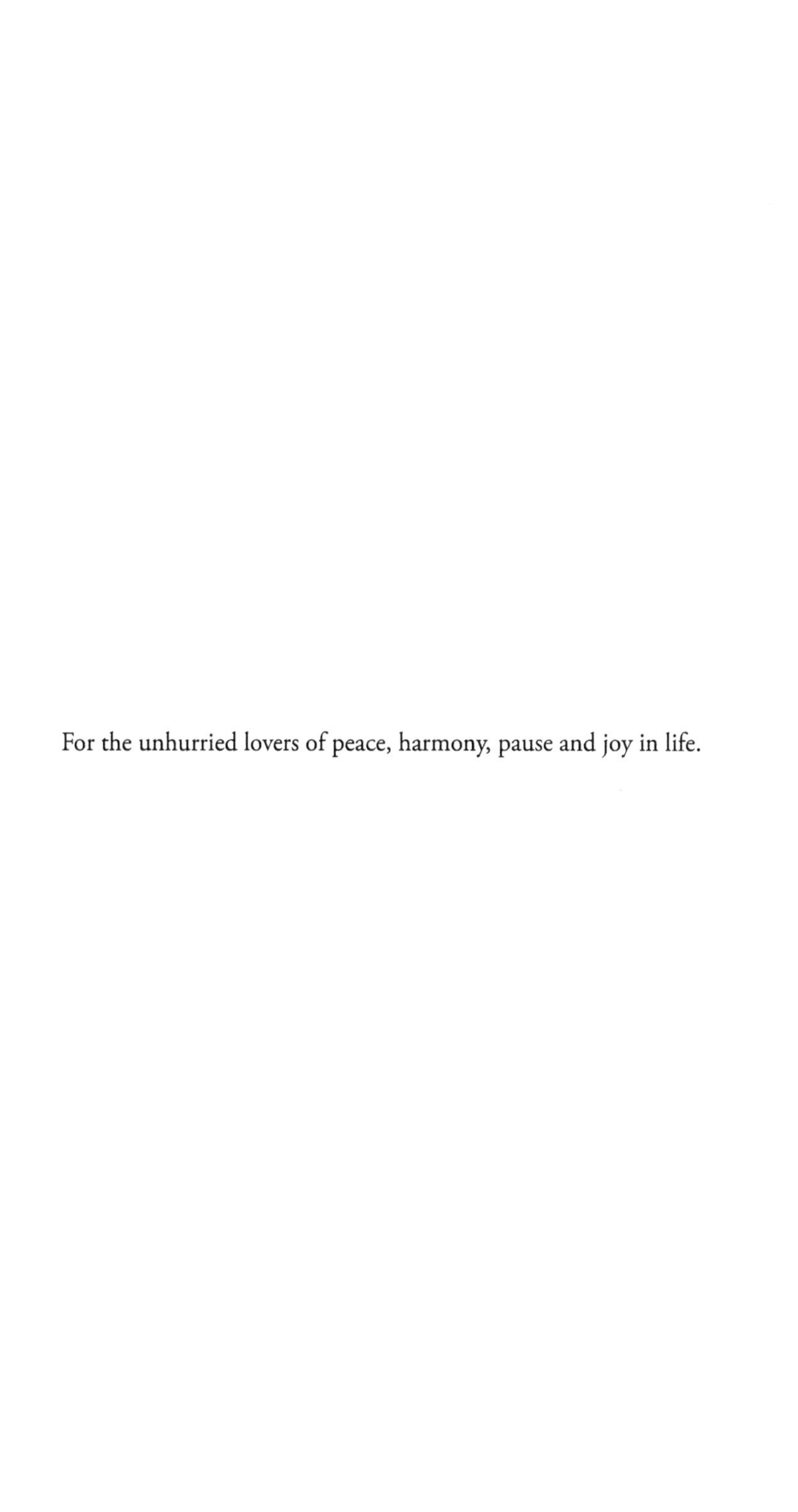

For the unhurried lovers of peace, harmony, pause and joy in life.

# Contents

# Contents

# Contents

# Foreword

James E. Faust: "A grateful heart is a beginning of greatness. It is an expression of humility. It is a foundation for the development of such virtues as prayer, faith, courage, contentment, happiness, love, and well-being."

Isn't it romantic beyond words? Come out of the stiff-faced prose of life. It squeezes you too tightly. Delve into the open charms of poetry. There is freedom for exhilarating escapades.

No guys no, I am not asking you to go out there and be a starving *shayar*. Expect money from other mundane occupations. Modern manmade system leaves you with countless opportunities to make mullah. All I am asking you to do is to get in league with harmony, rhythm somewhere deep in you, which is just a replica of the cosmic harmony of stars and galaxies going cyclically as per the ultimate law.

Plato: "Every heart sings a song, incomplete, until another heart whispers back. Those who wish to sing always find a song. At the touch of a lover, everyone becomes a poet."

And as love caresses you, you are supposed to turn a poet. And your life a poem. A life lived poetically nourishes your soul. The prose approach to life is simply to earn the conveniences to support you materially.

Niels Bohr, lost in the endless evolution of atomic possibilities at the subatomic level, surrendered his hardcore matter of factuality and turned a dreamer: "When it comes to atoms, language can be used only as in poetry. The poet, too, is not nearly so concerned with describing facts as with creating images."

If life appears stale and boring, you have got to blame your own self. For you lack imagination in not seeing the endless colors and splendorous charms lying around.

A bit of poetic daydreaming detoxifies the crammed brain because with poetic imagination, a sense of beauty pervades your being, putting all other pinching realities of life at bay.

You have got to believe me, the Big Bang was a poetic moment. If not for the infinite possibility of rhyme and rhythm, me and all you out there won't have been enjoying this beautiful unfolding of things and phenomena according to self-sustaining laws.

Without the seed of poetry there won't be any prose. Just like without the tiny seed there won't be a tree. The canopy, the full foliage of the tree, is just an extension of the dream lying with its realistic potential inside the small seed. The elaborate network of trunks, branches, twigs, flowers, fruits and leaves is nothing but a commentary on the small poetic seed. So all ye wannabe writers of a good life story, nurture the poet in you, who understands the value of pause in life, who moves slowly to watch everything, sight and smell everything. Whose senses are open to the inclusive interplay of wonderful harmonies of the supreme song, the universe, *the one song*.

The brushstrokes of poetry softly touch the soul without disrupting its restful muse and bring out the nuggets of love, compassion, harmony and peace. If you are poetic in nature, you have the potential to be anything because all these elaborate extensions of your life, your dreams, your professional and personal goals, your milestones, the world around you, all these and more are nothing but a reflection of that poetic pure seed.

Being poetic is being the master of all the best-ever possible emotions as a human being. No wonder love and poetry are almost synonymous. Poetry is the common soul of all the art forms. It's a smiling and loving approach to life, not just rhymes on paper. It's about being in tune with the soft chimes of your soul. It is impossible to visualize an unpoetic artist. It's impossible to have an unpoetic visionary. It's impossible to have an achiever who did not dream poetically.

Poetry is the womb that mothers all that has ever been loved and appreciated by the mankind and Mother Nature. To be poetic is to love. You taste godliness by being poetic. The mankind has pictured heaven just as a huge poetic dream. All the myths, gods and goddesses are marvelous poet philosophers and poet soldiers. So learn to be a poet. Love yourself as a poet. You will find love shielding you with its soft power making you the best of a human being.

Irony is that our language is a poor carrier of the ultimate truth. But ultimate truth is best summarized by the word 'love'. Within written styles, poetry lets loose its open invitation to invite truth. Even though it smiles hazily, yet it has its charms; some poetic outpour to reach out to the ultimate with your love.

# 1. Life

It is good that
we must cultivate dreams,
But most often
man's uncertainty and destiny's certainty screams
to shatter them to pieces.
We, though must hope
to evade the deadly anchor's drop,
It is our futile, and not so futile, duty to
carry the life's ship through heaving waves,
Wonderful! So many winds one braves!
Like smouldering coal in the hull
the passion ever craves,
The tiny flicker braves
against the mightiest swathes of stormy dark,
Storms, meanwhile, play against the timber strong,
In the wooden frame, but, many dreams throng,
And enjoy the journey, though, unfinishable and long!
Time's worms eat the timber,
And stealthily doth eventuality limber,
to sneak through the destiny's holes,
Longly piled up agony of the storm furiously rolls,
Carried thou so far and wide;
tattered are those soles.

We carry a mountainous bulk of hopes
encased in some ash and tear drops,
How meticulously time thrashes its harvest,--
From buxom ripe fruits
it reaps only peelings and stones,
From life's crop
death reaps only the lifeless drop,
The majestic reaper
wants but few grains of soil
from all the juicy, lifeful, thriving tissues.
Still, we have to live
and we need to hope
till that final mop,
We know that the slate will be
cleaned up after all,
But we have to play our part in life's ball,
For crammed will be the hall
tomorrow as well,
When in other bodies life will dwell.

# 2. Conversation with a Stranger

One day he asked someone hiding inside
the bodily façade like a fugitive,
'Who are thou?
And why despite all the architectural negativities
people define thou positively?'
From its unreachable deep cellar
that someone raised its germ-free, disinfected voice,
'I am the exiled one without choice,
While the bones and the flesh around me
in worldly spotlight rejoice,
I just take the ordained backseat
and watch the game of
birth, survival, struggle and death
played inside the castle on the shaking stage.'
'Don't you feel perplexed by the passing days?'
Again the query was voiced,
'Don't you feel bad or ever you rejoiced?'
It answered in a heavy, impassive tone,
'Thy gimmick cannot shake my throne,
In the timeless shades I spend my time here
and when the castle will be broken
the death squad will find the door open,

Away I'll fly with the figures of
deeds and misdeeds to the final court,
and if it is found short,
again I'll be exiled.
It has been like this for thousands of years,
but I never rejoice at new birth
nor weep at death and shed tears,
My book lies in mighty primordial hands
and the player to settle scores
changes with worldly trends,
I am the same forlorn, exiled child
of the majestic, mighty father,
It's a never-ending game perhaps,
A tiny cog on the chessboard of creation,
Let's see how high and mighty you make the castle,
Void will then gobble the tone and stars!'

# 3. Whom Should I Blame?

What we do and what we don't,--
Maybe it is our choice,
Or maybe the hands of providence
guide or misguide?
Don't know
whether it is our action's rejoice,
or partisan fate's prejudice?
Stealthily we try to ensure
the credit for the good falls in our own bag,
And if things go wrong
our stage-manages throng
to put all blame on the old hag.
Whatever we may think of ourselves,
We're, but, the good- or bad-chanced kids
of the parental—earthly and other worldly—topsy-turvies,
If not so,
What person is there to wish
directly his doom;
Which life's light voluntarily seeks
to be extinguished to gloom?
Still—less directly and more indirectly—many
against their will are brought to the wrong end,
Where the expected destination

does not exist not even in name;
Where the undoing sweeper chuckles in all its fame,
And the half-willed animal
gets tethered to a peg for a chained tame,
Then follows the great game,
Many try to put each other to blame.
It is but a futile mockery,
Mere verbosity cannot bust
the secret of that trickery.
Ever-lorn to justify ourselves,
Many-a-time we put the blame
squarely on the destiny's elves,
saving just digestible morsels for ourselves,
And feed mammoth dose of
unwanted garbage to the uncomplaining lady.
What does it matter
if the blame lies with us
or it is borne by the
speeding wheel's crush,
The loss, after all, is a loss,
Whoever is the causing boss.
To me, either both of us go scot free,
Or both are put under the accuser's glee!

# 4. Victory

O thou poor lady of rich virtues
and big but spent eyes,
Thy rosy, soft, tempting lips
bear the blood-drawn scar of a
timeless, incessant, ever-greedy, lusty kiss;
On your fair cheek, tireless pursuer's mouth;
Muck with saliva and pitiless, sadistic hiss;
Your majestic head,
heavily diamonded with uncountable,
innumerable, romping homes and wins;
Smartly, smirkly are tied under this crown,
thy mercilessly, heedlessly, heartlessly tresses
tampered by the fingers committing sins;
Thy firm, upright breasts have been
bobbed to excitement so many times
that stonily they no longer feel the lover's lick,
They now feel the pathetic kid's sickly blood-suckling.
I wonder after so many love-romps, intercourses,
love-makings, rapes, smotherings and sex games
—the victories—
what thou feel in the area of focus of such tireless passions!
Is it still the titillating sexual ecstasy,
or every endeavour is as repulsive

as the stealthy, predatory approach of a cowardly hyena?
Thou were once the Goddess of the realm of
commitment, excellence and diligent striving-forth,
But for thousands of years,
wars were lustily ravaged against thy beautiful body
and thy blissful skin was bombarded with
human passions and pestilence.
If the lofty destination all but becomes
final steps of the mucking path,
Mud will definitely cling at its own apron,
As the stained devotee falls at its feet
after all those gutted baths,
And in its insurmountable helplessness
the Goddess of yore has been turned into a prostitute,
Though they still worship it in its old physical avatar,
But that soul banished and left destitute,
The herculean endeavours and efforts
of these throbbing masses
go on squeezing from all sides,
Thou in a tight corner,
Dressless and pitted against the wall;
Only that small, soft hand hides thy honour,
Thy Godly spirit now driven back to the
edge of a fearsome precipice,
Thou are no longer the Queen,
for thy own fate seems
worth decidable by the throw of a dice.

The poor lady now stands all exhausted;
Tattered, battered, bruised at the lowest tide,
The most coveted, prized virgin
now sulks like a dejuiced, unsuitable fruit
ready and waiting to give its stone and hide,
What can I get from you O poor lady?
Thy treasure trove is all but famished now,
You are left with just
monstrously compromised Satan's diamonds,
Even my beautifully courting pursuit
will seem a poor robbery and loot,
So here I step aside
from the blood- and treachery-rutted path,
and think of some long-drawn, circuitous path
that can take me
—after a life-long hard-worked journey—
to an isolated place
that may provide me thy pure, unstained sight!

# 5. Dark Shelter

Too far and deep I have gone into the pit of gloom,
And lost in the cavernous folds of the impending doom,
Even the brightest big suns now appear too far,
Faint stars these now and just flash their inspiring rays,
Feeble raylets reaching me cannot take out the ship caught in treacherous bays,
I know the futility of the beckoning light,
Even in its brightest folds outside, hope was always out of sight,
Now i go deep into my night,
With nobody as a witness to my plight,
All cherished dreams out of sight,
A wingless bird that tried to fly but then crashed from its struggled height,
Now I just silently walk into the dark hold of my night,
Alone
and forlorn,
Musicity of my soft moan,
Carrying me into hitherto unreachable zone!

# 6. Dark Shades under Light

It has been months since
I last lit my faith's lamp,
So many days have passed since
prayers chimed in my dark den's air damp,
My meditating self,
Now gives atheistic yelp.
Lost my faith!
Lost my prayer!
Lost my rituals!
Lost my meditative trance!

# 7. Hope Melting out of Frigidities!

There is light beyond the deepest dark depth,
There is a bright day after the ghostly haunts of nightmarish night,
After a barren famished fight there is a blossomed spring delight,
After pining pangs of separation there is a worthy end to the desperation,
After crashing in the gutters there is a surge and rise to bathe in holy waters,
After crying convulsions on the lips, a smile takes honeyed sips,
After the last defeat, still there is an undying urge to accomplish the feat,
Even when blind with despair, there is hope hiding and cajoling somewhere,
Even in hate love still lurks somewhere!

# 8. Self-defined World

The Spring's traces last,
Hot summers approaching fast,
Languid notes in the air,
A solitary bird's forlorn chirping for musical share,
Drowned in stillness
this late morning bright and fair,
Sky's dull blue,
Overhanging the earth in paling hue,
But a smaller world is there,
The overall lethargy cannot reach where,--
In its self-defined world
in a corner tiny,
The luscious wild flower
still stands brave and shiny!

# 9. Being with the Self!

I know life has rejected me,
And death when will accept me
that time is yet to be!
Till then, O Sufi, is there any light to see?
Yes fella!
It's in being with those who have been discarded by fate,
Who have laboriously scrawled and scribbled lifelong
but still have a clean slate;
It's in smiling with innocent dawns;
It's in basking in the sunny charms of forlorn lawns;
It's in the faded twinkle of distant stars;
It's in saying goodbye to the intrigues of my own internal wars;
It's in being with me,
And the way it is, let it be!

# 10. Lovebites

The poisonous black coils hiss
and entangled in fanged loops go for a kiss.
Two glossy-black slithery bodies
lost in the fearsome quagmire of poisoned passion
eat each other's identity in some unheard fashion.
The venomous fangs,
Lay bare their monstrosity,
making the moments vicious, stealthy, dangerous.
The tongues of death
nastily sway to a mysterious song,
It is like brutal soldiers of death
marching on a bloody path endlessly long.
It is like death dancing:
Its poisoned lips heaving, pushing its mighty pout
against the innocent, pure face of mortality.
Pitted against the cataclysmic forces of death,
the lovely pink sheen on the pristine face prevails.
Its softest brace breaks thc hardcst stones.
The fierce aura suddenly bids time to stay still,
to extinguish its fire at the acme:
the pleasure-topped hill.
The love prevails,
The horrible storm loses its restless travails

in the hazily lit mellowness of ecstatic surrender:
Defanged, depoisoned.
They are now just two beautiful creatures.

# 11. The Old Bull and the Dead Wood

I'm an old bull,
My rock-hard bones heave and pull
the rickety cart,
I'm skinny but perfect in my belief
that I've to justify my morsels before I depart.
I carry a dead body that once was
a robust attire for some sylvan soul,
It was an honest being;
this sturdy, hard body,
It fulfilled all its duties without exception.
But then this is the age of vandals,
They can just vandalize only,
They axed it, chopped it.
I now carry the carcass
as the trophy of their triumphant glory,
I but silently mull over this murder story.
Delhi around me boasts of its mechanized colours;
cars, megamalls, skyscrapers,
westernized guys and gals,
and thousands of glamorous pitfalls.
Haa..wonder they can't do without me!
With salivated gusto

my laboured breathing eggs me on,
while my victimized skeleton creaks and bemoan.
The flyover is the challenge,
My owner beats my back like an enemy,
It is a treacherous task,
But it is my duty to carry the body
for its final rites,
otherwise someone will miss
many a drawing room delights.

# 12. Iron Lady

It is noisy chaos,
Delhi at its best,
Impatient horns, smoky guffaws,
tired engines, shouts, dust,...
The lotus, but, shines in the mud.
Pulling the carrier rickshaw she is unfazed,
Two kids, a goat, a bundle of poor provisions
safely in tow,
Like a valiant captain at the best row.
Clad in a dirty *saree*
she shines like a queen,
I don't think femininity had ever been
so illustrious in its sheen.
Meanwhile, madly mechanized world hisses,
But its lolloping tongue meekly kisses
the dirt on her hardened feet,
She pulls the rickshaw with pride
in full maternal heat,
Cramped for space she turns the tide,
The goat and the kids though panicked,
but the mother carries on the fight
in the traffic jam,
Fights for space with utmost grace,

and clears like a swiftest deer's brace.

# 13. The prisoner

I'm ragged old,
I was once the youth icon
of the fauna around me,
Delhi was far and nonthreatening then,
We just enjoyed its lights from a safe distance,
The city didn't seem at war with us,
But then it just spilled over,
Its bridges, roads, cemented pavements
ate into our innards,
I witnessed massacre of my near and dear ones,
I'm now caged in a high rise residential complex,
I'm just a poor banyan tree now,
Standing as an archaic symbol
in my cramped corner of this little park.
I go out of my way to give shade and cool air,
But I'm horrified and scared.
Even a kid picking a tiny pebble
to playfully hit my canopy
sounds like a terrorist hurling a deadly grenade.
So, against my nature
I'm always on guard,
crying for peace and mercy,
But it is too noisy around,

My mercy petitions fall on the deaf ears
of the stony facades standing haughty and proud,
I'm afraid any day the judgment
will arrive against me!

# 14. Encroachers

This thunderous beat of waves on the beach
tries to reach
the hardest core of the rocks standing
mute and sullen on the coast.
The sea and its maddening waves;
uproarious, stormy, and boastful most.
For years, its stormy passion kissed the rocky face,
The fury of its infatuation caught the unsoliciting
lover in a grasping embrace,
The rocks mellowed and crumbled as beach sand,
Once where there was land
now becomes the soft love bed
for the waves to shed
their gnashing fury on its soft grains,
where love sighs in gay abandon
and soft showers turn into torrential drains.
In this land—sea love pit—
a new passion gets lit,
Surrendered to excited storms
we forget all norms
and let loose waves
that break false rigidities and forced facades
build inside us for decades.

Waves to waves!
Rocks to rocks!
The sea just watches meekly
this sensuous storm on its bed:
The encroachers with all shame shed,
Its warning shouts ebbing away in distance,
as if afraid of this rival stormy surge
on the beach,
It recedes to save itself from this
huffing, puffing , grunting, tempestuous game.

# 15. Lady on the Canvas

When a painter paints his lady,
Even the colours seem ready
To sacrifice theirs and turn hers,
Vow, colours ebriated form a painted verse!
The brush too gyrates,
Softly, softly it narrates
His love tale,
Blossomed how a flower in a dale.
He, the love's portrayer,
His soul immersed in a deep prayer,
Her features emerging,
Aha, love through his hands oozing!
Those eyes now ogle at him,
Deep, deep to the soul's dim,
And his eyes at hers,
Goes on painting the verse!
When the love is fully faced,
Brush suddenly stopped and fingers braced
The pretty face eager for a praise,
Fallen sage got the colour erase.
The funny lady on the canvas,
Stared at him with extreme alas,
And furiously said,

Dear, have you gone mad!

# 16. Sea's Home-coming

Waves sway in the rocky bay,
Sea in this small playground plays,
Such vastness engulfed amidst rising rays!
Father comes to the daughter from far away,
While, scattered, toyed, rocks lay
Numb to 'father-child' who gyrates,
And daughter's lullaby exhilarates,
Sky, meanwhile, claps its cloudy array.
O visitor waves,
Existence-lorn, thou come
Here for a homely swash,
Peep playfully inside coastal caves,
Bring aquatic gifts for some,
Along with gusts of air fresh.

# 17. Night Song

O Cuckoo, thrown destitute,
Singst thou now in nigritude:
The beautiful rhymed song,—
For whom? Wait who hung
In adopted nest and parents deceived;
Mistook as nestlings conceived.
O singer of conceited bravery,
On this night dreary,
Drive they competitors out
To eat whole food; become stout.
O foolish singing mother,
I blame thee not; migratory, wind flown,
Spring abandoned thou either,
Summer gusts left thee alone,
Now, like nightingale thou singst
A long song for the night:
Feel I thy Florence nurst;
The rhymed heal over destruct,—
A day's war we swampt,
Thou now wander with the lyrical lamp.
How unmotherly thou art!
Not to pour ditty whole
Upon thy eggs waiting hatch,

Like black Goddess, thou dart
Across the blackness as the mother sole,
Lulling lolly thine match,
The life song over night's camp,
Thou keep life's lamp
Burning with thy awake,
Please, keep singing for our sake.

# 18. The Nature in Love

The singing vales and flowery dales,
Away, somewhere in nature's cradles,
Dreams open arms, with all charms,
Come here, come here! Worry not falls and waddles!
The place in isolation, with Godly intuition,
Too excited to meet someone!
Come dear! Come dear! Don't thou hear
And remember that fun.
The musical rivulet, and thy hut,
By fullest heart they call,
And the air awaits with thy breath's share,
While the clouds still remember that playing pal.
Trees sway with breeze,
It whispers patience in their ears,
'Come he will, on this hill,
In dreams, thy call he hears.'
Little pathway, companion on that day,
Embraces those footsteps still,
Hums that song, sung in shadows long,
Where is he? Asks a cloud passing the hill.
Wild beauty of yore; opens heart's door,
Remained I loveless for too long,
Then thou came, with thy love's tame,

Resonates here now always the love song.
Thus the lovely vale, falls in love's dale,
The love-lorn lady; silent beauties moan,
Dreams moments those, blossomed when love's rose,
Come, come! What purpose serves the beauty alone?

# 19. The Night in Revolt

The sky is too starry today!
As if the night too wants a new ray,
Whitish shine of mother milky-way,
In her lap numerous stars play.
Stars visible to the horizon,
As if the night has arisen,
In revolt against the dark; with a vision,
While, the darkness browbeats for the treason.
Like martyrs the aerolites go,
As if to show:
Burn brightest, but not bow
Before the dark, which destiny casts over the show.
Their escapades over blackness' chest,
Aha the life lived best!
Too much fiery light, then salvation rest,
Break they out of binding circle; much to destiny's detest.
The sky with its vault starry,
While, the dark seemst wary,
Its agitated darkness scared of the enemy hoary,
Oh! Feeblest shine of farthest star seemst so fiery!
Thus the night glows in revolt,
Depredations in every nook corner, to bolt
The dark behind the strongest door, and halt

Its march; shines every eye with a colt.

# 20. Enlightened Moon

How mysteriously the moon
Was shining last night!
Dim, oblate, struggling half,
As if a fallen hero
Trying to arise for another fight.
The great souled!
Waging still a righteous war,
Though shadows were subduing light,
It did not seem faint hearted,
Went on fighting, without caring
For the infamy about the look,–
The popular esteem of a full moon.
How divine was its even-mindedness!
Exempt from pleasure and pain,
Loss and gain,
Thus, free from the grasp of opposites,
This scion of warrior class
Went on with its dispassionate work,
While, the sense objects around,
Scattered sleepily across the ground,
Find this truthful seer,
Quite unfathomable and worthy of jeer!

# 21. Too Far the Birds have Gone!

Where have the birds gone?
Too many of them used to roam
The sky over the villagers' head,
Yesterday, I saw a couple too sad,
Are many of them dead?
The parrots, pigeons and sparrows;
Humanity's flowery arrows,
Have they gone too far?
Away! Where man is not at war
With the nature, –
Awaits where future
Like a self imposed zoo,
While, vast treeless tracts rue
For the natives now exiled.
Sometimes, the winged visitors come
To solace the mighty tree gone dumb,
The houses now without corniced crevices,
Oh! The niches, holes from the wall
Enter the plastered souls,
Architect, thou grow too tall,
Too spacious and monotonous fouls,
Accommodate which only human,

Oh! Why thy constructive acumen
Sprouts only from the nature's grave?
The birds thus try to reach
Where we still have not,
To escape our civilizing shot,
The chirps and the singing shrieks
Which the kids imitated to sharpen verbal beaks
Now die and fade out
Amidst all this urbanizing shout!

# 22. Journey with the Autumn

Autumn, become my friend,
Thou holding my hand,
Take me through the windfalls,
To help me forget my own tree's bereaving calls.
The tree where summer's ripenings,
Too fruity, heavy for the branch's likings,
The air through their fall singth,
While, thou make me follow thy grayish path.
'See not thy own windfalls',
Thou say, dodging thy falls,
And push me from my tree,
So that I become mourn-free.
And the autumn path brownish,
Summer's warmth vanish
Joyfully from fruits, leaves,
Vow! Fairy for its beauty not grieves.
Happily I run with thcc,
Away! Away! Where another season be,
Where trees glee with fruity prospects more,
Where snow melts to welcome the spring at its door.

# 23. Alas, the Orchid Too Far!

The rising rays fell upon a dream,
Shining future got upstream,
And expectations windily blown,
Nobody, meanwhile, listened destiny's scream.
How painfully he nourished that dream!
The sweaty toil to nurture
And water the bud for flowery future,
How rugged the chosen path seem!
The path to that
Lush green orchard,
For whom he went diehard,
While, the fate chuckling for a bet.
Went flowerily on the path,
Following the flower of life,
Alas, the 'predetermined' preparing its knife,
To cut the bud for its bloody bath.
Reached he when there,
With his feet all bloodied,
The bud lay already buried,
And the orchid gone for cemetery's bare.
God, why the sincerest efforts fail?
Perhaps, victory too loses

To huge efforts, which give it repeated bruises,
The unsung heroes, whom it doth hail.

# 24. Alas, the Spring Too Far!

Frigid fate gone to ferocious winters;
The winter with its frosty bite,
Shivers where warmth's might,
And failure lets loose its hungry hunters.
Aah, the ice cold reality!
So ruthless for vein's warmth,
And the forceful fist disarmth,
Lost is manhood of its valiant beauty.
The blizzards seem so frightful,
Oh! Superficiality crumbles deadly,
The avalanche hurries madly,
To follow the failure for its handful.
Long Ago the summer passed,
And autumn too with its windfalls,
The winter but seemst too harsh,
Will spring ever blossom where death danced?

# 25. A Rhyme Written Across the Jungle

The meditative flow
Of this small brook;
The waters serene and slow,
Move bearing a pebbled look.
The jungle seems
Spellbound by its beauty,
Like a lover dreams
About those curves and lips pouty.
And the trees
Watch the damsel with gleeful eyes,
Softest of the breeze,
Slow, slow the silent majesty flies!
A sparrow dips its small beak
Into the generous, smiling water,
Thirst goes away! And seek
Refuge where water doth falter.
This slim feminine Goddess,
Blesses everything with its soft touch,
Aha, extreme beauty seemst too modest!
This wild maiden is careless such.
Thus, the brook flows with its beauty,
In harmony with the time,

The universal flow doing its duty,
God, how great is thy flowing rhyme!

# 26. A Maiden's Living Painting

Heaven has just sprinkled green,
Wonder, if nature had ever been
Painted so monotonously!
Paddy, paddy everywhere, He says generously,
The greenish sweep sways,
Guess what the sun says?
Shy-eyed from that cloud's corner above,
Green-girdled maiden gives naughty shove.
And the clouds roam;
The love separating dome,
Prevent the full eye's glee,
Lover lost; his damsel on the flee.
Softly, softly comes the breeze,
So that time may not seize
The beauty gone motionless,
Nimbly flutters her dress.
Farmers paying tribute to Goddess green,
Remove wrong colours from the scene,
The devotees with painter's precision,
Go on working, working with a vision.
She, meanwhile, gallops across fields,
Giggling and air-heeled,

The virgin in its full bloom,
Would-be-mother, many fates lie in thy womb.

# 27. The Star with Endless Beauty

Full bloomed flower; beauty in shower,
Raining to drench, raining to drench!
To colour eyes dry, where colourless dreams cry,
Softly pacifying destiny's lynch.
Aha coloured rain, shooing away defeat's pain!
Forget everything, forget everything!
For heaven's sake, and take
Glimpse of the real being.
The petals soft, inspire aloft,
Live like me, live like me!
Make hay a day; worry not last ray,
Let life a flower be!
Give fragrance, without self's hindrance,
Multi-hue others, multi-hue others!
So, death when comes, a loser it becomes,
Everything already given, now what is gathers!
Glow thou beauty, it is thy duty,
To celebrate and congratulate even those who lose,
Godly appreciation, so that desperation
Does not become deadly noose.

# 28. Wild Beauty from Hills

The mighty river, in wintry shiver,
Warmly it flows; water motherly glows,
Majestic Goddess! Gay abandon and virgin fresh!
To wash the child; for aeons who guiled.
Comes cold air, to kiss the upper layer,–
Flautist around her lips, blowing musical whiffs,
Untamed beauty listens not, with mountains it fought,
Defeated broadest shoulders; sensuous curves ate boulders,
From far, far............ without distance's bar,
Thou walk everywhere; stop nowhere,
Like beauty nomad, who doesn't shed
Her heart's tear; which her freedom can't bear.
Lapping, joyous water; thy stony falter,
Thou, but, never fall, clear obstructions all,
Rock woes! Wins as a dewy rose,
Thy victorious path, for the sinner's bath.
Beauty wins, while proud father grins,
Daughter go on, and do not moan
Thy victory's incise; it is father's prize,
Take my worth, for the plain's mirth.
Timelessly it goes, like immortal rose,
For millions' sake, and take
Faith in full flow; save the sinking low,

Rest it doesn't take, till the final lake.

# 29. Deep, Deep! Water Exists Somewhere

He went on digging a well,
With his spirit valorous,
Deep, deep! For success smell,
His battle-song like divine chorus
Waxed the belief to most solid state,
Only to such heroes, God's emblems relate.
The water at unfathomable depth,
Still, hardest effort's divine force,
Kept him going and he never dejectedly slept,
Far, far! Soft light's mild source
Kept up this cloud-light's thunderous spark,
Vow, puritan at war with the dark!
Fighting he was from the God's side,
Against devil trying belief's downfall,
On his brave back Godhood ride,
Like an awful radiant ball,
To reach the goal, piercing earth,
And play with deepest water in mirth.
Volcanically he went,
Cleansing earth almost spiritually,
Digging, digging with back bent,
To reach water, somewhere gushing fully,

O thou free roaming soul,
For how long could escape thy goal?

# 30. The Music in Solitude

He just went on a long journey,
Which the soul lit up,
While, the matter's stern pride
Trying to stave off the fighter.
With his great heart glowing;
The living fountain of light,
Went on fighting the darkness,–
Heavenly luminary kindled this lamp!
Sacred mystery giving him safe passage,
From that bottom of appearance;
The sorrow-stricken bearance,
Aha, nobler destiny awaits somewhere!
The musical journey!
Music of word, heart and nature,
For that fountain of splendour,
Gushing heavenly at the infinity's fringe.
Traveller himself amuser and the amused,
Such is the inward symmetry,
His rhythmic footsteps with a song,
While, divinity sways to his tune.

# 31. Processing of Greatness

A fluty wail from the well of woe,
With angels playing harp softly above,
Dumb music from this most tragic tragedy,
Go on, Go on! Crown of mercy too greedy.
The tragic, saddened heart,
Where the lamp of longest pain burn,
Its light reaching transcendental eye,
And the oil of fallacy saying smoky bye.
Aah the ways of destiny!
Who can understand its allegory?
Why doth purest affection of human soul,
Gets crushed for the purest emblem of the whole?
Too far is heaven's corbel!
There sanctified souls dwell,
They sing, go to tragedy's depth,
For, without pain's awake, no one ever slept,
Perhaps, too vivid is pleasure after a long pain;
Golden glow of morning after night's rain,
The pure star in clearest sky,
After worst elements, now shining high!

# 32. Surrender

God! Here and now I surrender before thee,
Let fate onwards be
At war with the prime deity,
Let it draw all arrows from its kitty.
Surrender to the nectarine form,
God! Brave now thee, thy own norm,
For I have lost the battle,
And leave war for you to settle.
I bow before thy supreme grace,
As defeat proudly brace
The low held head,
While, all willpower gone dead.
Too loudly the victorious conchs blare,
And the defeated, wounded can't dare
To touch the weapons in dust lying,
For, winner's fatal most arrow still eyeing.
So many efforts butchered this macabre,
Aah! The annihilator with its tabor,
Its ghastly, nasty dance,
Gives me not the singlest chance.
God! Now I lie at thy feet,
And see how thou beat
Someone who fought so valiantly,

Fell then down silently.

# 33. The Hero

What if a man's might
Beats destiny's delight?
Like the aerolite,
In a cold dreary night,
Gives the brightest fight,
For the sake of light,
O the never ending aerolite!
Always too bright,
Defeating fate's sight,
Escaping its play site,
Where nothing holds tight,
And all fateless in their own right,
Paying a blissful rite,
To the destiny gone quiet,
Yes! There are some kites,
Which reach such heights,
Not to fall for earthly delights.

# 34. God's Child Playing

Once again I fall,
Fall on my knees,
Like a child after a ball,
And like father, God watches with please.
The mighty father sees
His cherub playing, learning,
Helps He not with every breeze,
Exclaims, 'Thou art just a starter darling!'
My mountainous tumbles,
To him just childish rolls,
And complaints just boyish grumbles,
Pacifies, 'Thou just play son, I worry about goals!'
And I go on playing
For the father's muse,
Constantly with spirits flying,
Till the teacher Himself rues.
The child thus goes
For the biggest of tries,
Yes! Smiles only a rose
After the branch gives many thorny cries.

# 35. Perhaps, It will Rain Today

The sky is overcast,
Grayish dark clouds
Ebriatedly stoop over,
Perhaps, rain will come,
And the birds anticipatedly fly,
Like the children turned all urchins;
Roaming across the streets,
Shouting with every thunder above.
The breeze comes cool,
To cool down the eagerness,
It whispers, wait, wait ye fellows,
Listen to that thunder,
God is certainly preparing water,
Listen to His bowl.
The trees wait with their wisdom;
Oh, the patience of decades, years!
While, the chirpy leaves, branches;
Childhood with its swinging moods,
Seems it as if an infant
Kicks grandpa's lap gone serene.
Only God knows when it will come,
When the dreams will reality become?

# 36. The Old man and the Night

The old man and the night,
Both of them lie awake.
His life fading out of sight,
Cough, meanwhile, doth a serious shake.
Lost out dark world around,
Times ago he was born,
The soul when got aground,
Old, old! Now it is other world-lorn.
Night is his companion now,
The day too hectic and bright,
So many of them swiftly passed, how?
Now the night comes, fades as the sight.
The night tries to bring sleep,
O mother, child sleepless for too long,
Time may come for a slumber deep,
And motherly it whispers a song.
Too much hurried was the day,
While the night has much patience,
The day only for the hair's grey,
The night doth die it black in silence.
The old man and his old mother,
Thus, stand by each other,

Stepmother will come with sunrise,
How will then cope the sun wise?

# 37. A Lovely Remembrance: Is it Love Still? Or Is Love Always for the Past?

Time was once,
When the flower was at its prime,
Lost love now only feign,–
Immortality which time can't maim!
What a great make believe!
Heart's no cause of yore,
Today, mind's cause to deceive:
Hence the lyrics required many more.
Celestial to remain in love
With love that once was!
By tongue it creates wave,
Ripples whose get lover 'pass'.
'Pass' in keeping flame alive
For others to see it
And credit for negating time's heave
Against the love lamp tenderly lit.
Where art fullest petals?
Which formed earthy beauty; love

Among vast stretches of vales,
Oof! Find them, now, afore toe.
Thy wide parted eyes,
Show now the angst;
Vision before them dies,
And thou laugh at the epitapher biggest.
Thy soft trysts in my arms
Make the pen stubborn,
Bent on creating charms,
But write they only lover's mourn.
At times thou had tears,
Brooked which thy rosy cheeks;
A flower flooded with fears,
Me now tryst only wordy shrieks.
Shaking lips when sent
Tremour theirs in mine,
Very same now hell bent
On paying lip service to that wine.
Then, thou sipped worries from my brow,
And the wrinkles there unfolded;
Luck seemed for a charming throw,–
Poet's lines, now, to be traded.
Those hot gasping whiffs
Formed warm passioned air,
Float, now, in cloudy ifs,
And the mystic sucking his share.
Aha that sleep thine

In the blessed lap mine!
Those thighs now seek pat,
Claim love's survival and bet.
Crossed I physical limits,
Souls merged to play games,
This lover now hits body
To show the soul lame.
Beloved, hardest I tryst
For thy aliveness in me,
Still, efforts to reach highest
On love scale always neigh.
Alas, thou art past now!
Historian, but, tries love still,–
New love seeds to sow
New love crop for some crazy will.

# 38. Ode to the Winter Sunset

The sunset on this small sandy plateau,
Agrestic fellows turn it in a paradise,
And the red rim with its salutary motto,—
Only from dust pearls arise.
Perfect becomes the nature's artistry,
As nothing changes to time's hurry,
Except sun amazed at one mystery;—
The lonely perch of a bird on a tree.
Happy homecomings of the birds,
Love where sinews the nests,
Purest friendship returns in herds,
While, the air as if in complete rests.
White shiny shrine under a *peepal*,
Enshrines faith in that lamp,
Burning perfect straight without flicker,
Perhaps, God, tonight, will lay here camp.
The crane couple passes with a cree.......k,
Echoing conch-shell alike,
Oh, the sacred chant which seek,
Blessings from the lamp; to light the whole night.
How calm the path seems!
No one to beat at its door

To reach the farthest of dreams,
And distance meaningless to this lazy-lore.
Sweet-sour berries amidst prickles,
Smile with their ripening orange colours,
On both sides; pathway's anklets
Give life to someone during the long hour.
Wheatlings lush green,
Pea's white flowers get a vegetative fold,
Lone farmer becomes keen
To pass watchful night in the cold.
And the sun tries to see
Inside his small hut,
God, let there be
Too much warmth for the frost's fret.
That misty wood of far,
Embanking the canal,
Seems too far
For the fading sun's rays all.
Look, how ascetically that dog walks
Along the lonely path's solitude!
Away, away from the settlers' barks,
How contently it lives on the farmers' gratitude!
Farmhouse on that gently uplifted fold,
Geology's smallest of dome
Shines to the day's rays old,
Seems as if paradise has got a home.
And when the sun starts

To go below the horizon,
Heavy hearted it parts
Away; where humanity's other half has arisen.

# 39. Flower and a Verse in Grave

I have a flower in my book,
A flower paged, levelled, worded
Among words of my verses,
Once its petals smiled fragrance,
Time was when it scented,
My poetry written around,
Like an epitaph now;
Verses of an instant's immortality,
Dropped which from time,
Form now flower's eulogy.
Life will dry out of the flower,
With the passage of time,
Dry it will become,
To be crumbled to pieces,
My words meanwhile
Chant its immortality.
The flower among pages,
The words and the verses,
And the book from start to end,
Meaningless and unreal,
Except the page flowery;
Two pages and a flower:

Oh the flowery grave!
Which lies buried there,
The flower or the verse?
Which one is the eulogy,
The nature's deflorating one,
Or the words from my pen?
Death seems in a puzzle there,
Start it should around the pointed stalk,
To sneak into compressed petals;
Or curve it should,
Around syllables, words, phrases.
A flower is there in my book!

# 40. Earthquake

The great hammer of God,
Fault in geology's abode,
Thousands loose balance to the strike,
And death, destruction prevail without fight.
The adjusting rocks
Spew out tremoring locks,
Which win over walls faithful,
And macabre clapping all joyful.
Aah! The roofs which sheltered,
And never bartered
The family's fate,
Now, crush all of them in sadistic hate.
The debris around,–
Mass graves surround
Still struggling soufflés,
Alas! The rescuing hand only baffles.
Infant's softest bones get crushed,
Why death only brushed
Aside mother from its reap?
Oh her eyes! Even tears weep.
If nature itself brings destruction,
Then who would auction
For the beautiful dreams,

Dreams which now die amidst screams!
Whom should we blame?
The nature playing its accidental game,
Or the fault lies with its child,
In rising too high with his knowledge mild.
How secretly nature plans
Its mystery to enhance
The unknown about it!
How ruthlessly soft petals get hit!
Someone's eyelids refuse
To come down and thus loose
The singlest moment of finding love lost,
The eyes which once glittered most.
Where'd so many soul go?
Wait ghostly in a row
To have the final rest,
Mutilated lies the body dearest.
Aah! Painful and fearful death,
For long it hath
Its wait for elders' body system strong,
Now, clutches its prey on foot wrong.
Human settlement song,
Which for long
Sang with its social source,
Turned, now, mourning by nature's force.
Courtyard flowers which once smiled
Along with the owner's child,

Now, they lie rumbled;
Child and the flower in concrete crumbled.
Worst kind of death's artistry,
Oh! Wanton most spread out cemetery,
Lives still alive; lie buried,
How ghastly death hurried!

# 41. The Caravan Moves Further

The windy air of fading February,
Frost beaten leaves finally give over.
Still, trees happy as spring hover in the air,
Withdraws winter as if in a hurry,
Inside pond, bright rays seem to marry
The dazzling waves; a sparkling pair,–
Passionate kisses in the starry shining layer,
Seeing which the winged visitors doth worry.
Oh! How unemotionally winter passes!
Like that gypsy caravan preparing to go away,
Gone will be the winter with gypsy damsel;–
Two heartless lasses
Will go along a lone pathway,
Away, away! Where autumns dazzle!

# 42. Ageless Flower

The spirituous wine,
How it addicts the adolescence!
Intoxicated heart, then, pine
For a flower awaiting florescence.
Most hallucinating is this
Heart's spirit,
Head goes all amiss,
And soul suddenly becomes bereft.
Divine potion's first taste,
Pleasure-garden's immortal flower,
Fade which not to time's haste,
Occupy heart's corner forever.
And after a long, long time,
Grave finds something still sublime!

# 43. A Long, Long Journey

A lone man was walking somewhere,
Along the secluded path's solace,
Brave walk to some distant place,
Eyes had tear,
As step-motherly fate never hear,
While, the only prize of his long race,
Jewelled his brow with grace,
Still, the destination nowhere near.
Looked it like a journey to infinity,
The only success of the footsteps
Was the maintenance of their pedigree,
Destiny followed to wipe them out without pity,
And the failure waited for momentary lapse
By the man, to fill its belly hungry.

# 44. A Name which has'n Written in the Air

Death, what a patient game
Thou play throughout life!
A life filled with strife,–
Thou always keep thy dark fame.
The life desperately tries to live,
Thou but grab a hideout
In its territory to blowout
The final flicker trying a survive.
How meaningless thou make
Everything about life's craving!
Oh, the name seemst all fake,
After its matter thou annihilate.
Someone, perhaps, understands the futility;–
Of a name written on water,
Still, it has the trivial most existing utility,
There are names which even the air deter.
The name so lifeless,
That it forgets itself,
With whom fate creates such a mess
That even death fears itself.
What death means to such a name?
Meaningless it doth seems,

How can it? There is nothing to maim;
Where there is none of lively dreams.

# 45. To the Solitude

The jungle and its solitude,
As if a destitute;
Alone and forlorn,
But happy to be born!
Silence rustles through twigs,
While, wilderness wispily digs
The deepest grave for its opposite,
And peace doth invest in wind-fallen deposit.
Away, away it seems,
Far away! Thus dreams here
Smile like a reality,
Same dreams, which suffocate in a city.
Like a mystic gone serene,
Environment here had been
Meditating from the yore,
While, rain poured with heavenly lore.
Like a lass too shy,
It doth try
To preserve its chaste privacy,–
Shrink away from any gaze lusty and lacy.
Wonder if everything here goes
On awake or enjoy perpetual sleepy dose!?
Perhaps, both enjoy synchronism,

Aha! The heaven without any antagonism.
Love oozes here without paired chemistry;
The love purest in history,
As everything here is a born lover,
And will remain such forever.

# 46. Ode to a Scientist (Stephen Hawking)

The wonderful concept of cosmos!
Do you know where lies the boss?
The one related to relativity,
Always attracting souls to its gravity.
The forces of nature;–
Consciousness where pervades the matter,
And the space-time continuum
Zeroing on our illusionary vacuum.
The defined part of universe:
Luminary physicist's verse,–
Beyond bigness in celestial bodies of the whole,
And lesser than compactness inside a black hole.
Still, human spirit takes quantum jump,
For moments few we dump
God as the possessor of all mystery,
And try a taste of the unknown's chemistry.
Theories are what they are,
Spirit, perhaps, at war
With the matter,
One goes only for another's better.
Reality but always one step ahead,
The ultimate expansionist is, perhaps, glad

To be symbolised as the God pious,
While, a lamp burns as faith on reality's dais.

# 47. Ode to the Winter

The winter pouts its fishy full,
Shiver as we beneath clothing and wool,
It jerks its foggy locks,
Fed up with chilly love, ye agrestic folks.
The mornings, with Silver Goddess
Spraying silver amidst the greens,
Feathers and furs get drenched,
Dart as birds across tiniest droplets.
And the trees seem so stoic;
Immortal shades from His brush,
Whom misty mortality fail to crush,
Vow, as if inspiring spirit from the gothic!
Look how the rural damsel goes!
As if dew diamonds a perfect rose,
Her salad gyration at misty dawn,
Anklets jingle to her music own.
Birds fly in the foggily-low-sky,
Earlier they took autumnally sigh,
For, too high seemed the teasing blue,
Now the flight without any rue.
The noon with a milky smile,
Like a bride after first night
Comes out dreamy and royal,

Others, while, enjoy her facial delight.
Aha the light breeze!
Steals dew diamonds from the leaves,
The airy-fairy, it doth tease,
Frees as it the beauty from the seize.
How wonderfully the day weds its night!
The crimson setting behind the mist,
Intoxicated gets the light,
Worries not the loss, as the couple kisst.
Night fog veils the stars, –
Millions shy beauties
Cajole the dark-misty-lover below,
Whose stoic chill gives a look of neglect harsh.
And how lonely the night feels,
As everything takes a shelter,
Like an orphan it tries to enter
A homely warmth in some corner.
How sleep prospers under the quilt!
The sleep fed by the bodily warmth;
Humanity energising itself,
As myriad dreams get built.
But, also the merciless cold
For the calf and the old,
Both cold-preyed and hold
Their souls inside life's fold.

# 48. Ode to the Early Winter

Autumn thus goes for the early winter,
Coolness now starts to tinker,
Topsy-turvy like an anchor,
It takes hold through its lazy days,
When the sun with its cooling grey rays,
Sprays amusing tender maze.
A new canvas on easel for painting:
Farmers go working as if hunting,
Paddy's brown sweep vanish to nothing,
And the barren fields get new beds,
Such a soft soil for the numerous heads
Of wheatlings, to prop up for survival breads!
Look autumn's leaves brown!
Finally, foliage gets them thrown
From the deciduous with a shivery frown,
While the winter sings a lullaby,
As if to sleep a baby:
'Too much thou played with summer's gaiety'.
Winter flowers blossom bold,
Lo the dahlia, petunia and marigold!
Wonder, soft petals fear not cold!
And feathered friends from distant arrive,

As if only here lives thrive,
Ducks fly V-shaped to nature's drive.
Rosy pastor, tailor bird and wagtails,
Painted stork, painted duck and common quails,
Because those wintery hails
In mountains force their sojourn here,
And same winter will take care
Of the visitors; whom season's scold not dare.
Mynah, drongo and ecstatic barbler,
Depict they cool-spirited farmer,
The air now bothers not the above 'warmer',
Its sulphureous ebriety doth sweep
The hairy velvety grass and keep
The intoxication perpetuated to the deep.
The egrets fly drollingly,
In the air blowing genteelly,
The air! As if its spring coming courteously
With its flowery shiver,
Yes! It is airy-fairy's spring here,
While, ebriated birdies fly as its flowers.
Such are the days of early winter;–
Fog, mist, dew, cold quietly enter,
Robustness, meanwhile, makes a small banter,
Vow, the invigorating Goddess smiles!
Blessing of wellbeing for miles,
While, the autumn goes for annual exiles.

# 49. Ode to an Early Winter Afternoon

The early winter afternoon singths
A rosy song for the balmy day,
The lyricist with littlest lines,
Whose beauty shines with silvery sunny rays.
Stoic storks having Spanish siesta,
While her cooings voice floral pink,
Oh, the snaily standstill fiesta!
The sages, guess what they think?
The sky's muse from above,
With fancy-lorn eyes,
Bless-lorn it doth bow,
Vow! Small sashaying misty blessings.
And the evening all fancy-free!
Because whatever we can imagine
Becometh real with a glee,
With luxuriating steps she doth begin.
Spread out emotional landscape,
Protruding paw in friendship,
Its wild instinct nobody can escape,
And congratulating passes fresh air's whiff.
The softy with its soft words
To her–the love-lorn farmer girl,

Whose fun and floridity buds
Open like a robust-hued pearl.
What a delicate weather it is!
As if clime is opening its taste buds,
Bravo be the beauty's bliss!
Petal power smiles above the muds.
Oh the evening like a chubby child;
Eye catcher and pleasantly plump,
Half listens to the sun's mild
Request for the reddish slump.
The evening with such rhythm
As the feministic ease of a belly dancer,–
The soul-stifler to its fathom;
Wheezing meteor by the curvy winker.
Therapeutic it seems
To the day's bumps and bruises,
The day which wailed thinly, now beams
Gossipy; leisure-lorn it cruises.
Too quiet like serenest shower;
The fair hussy without being fussy,
Like Chrysanthemums for Christmas
Show no heed to the bee's hurry.
Everything as if meditation brained,
And heart with all its waters coloured,
While foxy logic all drained,
As if a cradle from heaven gets lowered.
And when the night starts to fall,

Vanishing paradise doth it seem, aye!
While, the paradise giving a call,
'Say me not a weepy-eyed bye'.

# 50. Single Beauty for All

Like a lover this gentle breeze
Touches and then whisks slowly away;
Away to that flower and appease
Its beloved by soft petal's sway.
I sense this flirting beauty's charm;
Hilarious like a fairy gone drunk,
Cold I feel; while its passionate love warm
Everything around, for it has turned so frank.
Aha the merrymaking as if wined!
So many love bites from the maiden;
Too many! And all of them find
A different lover in the single beauty hidden.
Go on, O thou seductive houri,
For I count for nothing but a crazy lover's fury.

# 51. The Carpet Maker

Who can understand the mysteries of life,–
Thrown entropy like a pack of cards:
Disarrayed, disjointed, unpatterened type,
And shreds we organise for some rewards.
Succeed when we in something,
We grin as destiny's maker,
And if blow sinews away for nothing,
Chide destiny as the breaker.
If something precious is found on the way,
For valiant foot's victory we hiss,
And if legs struggle for the destination far away,
Fault lies with His wish.
So, the question grows bigger till end,
When, perhaps, death answers with a helping hand.

# 52. Summered Sparrow

O brownie sparrow small,
Thou fly with harvested dust,
Aware thou become of nest's call,
Her beak pants there with maternal trust.
Collect thou grains lost,
Noon time numbing heat; feathers beat
Upon peasant's toil; now thy host,
Thy valiant jumps and crafty feat.
Sun-baked grains hardest,
Still, thou cut with cordial *chutts*,
Sawed *Shakti* makes thee worthiest;
Kitchen, water and eatable nuts.
Over parched terrain thou dart alone,
Agile, vibrant more, despite water gone.

# 53. Life Flirts

Here I come to this small puddle,
Sit on its shore and feel water,
Scorching sun, wind hot, dust fly,
Oasis driven, I but ogle at the water only.
Boiling pot it seems; vapourising layers,
Few lives drop in it suddenly:
Sparrows few wet feathers there,
Lifefully they escape the rising dead water.
With my feet in water and
Chin domed upon hands beaming knees,
I see life flirting in dying water,
Skin hard, meanwhile, feels molecules going up.
'Life is here or there?' I think,
Mirages over ponderous small waves,
Oh Yes! Water dies but plays still;–
Flirt we have with life; death weds in the end.

# 54. That Unknown Place

Some deep forest it was somewhere;–
Oak, ash, elm, beech, sycamore,
Embracing, climbing vines dare
Heights where love opened door.
There love need not be made,
Rather it existed stoically,
And not as desire's aid;
Stepped it out naturally, not frolically.
There leaves shone full green,
And grew pale after youth's bloom,
Floated then downwards unseen,
Ha! O death, thy own doom!
The place, creator of its own destiny:
Accident, predetermination there fail,
Basks timeliness of instants many!
Wonder, whether they ever caught time's tail?
Silent to the very core of silence,
Save some silent symphony by
Some bird larking by some unknown sense;
Noise of every sort there die.
Too unfamiliar a place,
Even to the sun partially known,
Curiously, thus, passes its face,

Doubting its fatherhood own.
Cloud crops fall into a world;
A world which its geography fathom not,
And in rumble-tumble they get rolled
Without hurt; Aaha! Cradle-caught.
The place where past seemed so evident,
Still present so independent!
And future with much secure accent,
Heavens! None from the trio lost with head bent.
Distance found itself unitless
Before the spread of that place;
Who can measure utter bliss?
Greenery that perplexed its face.
It looked as the centre of all goodness on earth;
As if God Himself comes there sometimes,
And rejuvenate all that mirth,
Persists which there as heavenly rhymes.

9 798887 042596

Printed by Libri Plureos GmbH in Hamburg,
Germany